"Shims and Shams"

"Shims and Shams"

June Magnuson

Published by Melissa Magnuson-Cannady, William Cannady, and Chris Magnuson

Printed by Lulu Press, Inc., www.lulu.com

Come, walk with me through time. We will laugh and cry together, and when the journey is done, know that hope springs eternal and we never walk alone.

Enjoy,

Jura Magnuson

Contents

Forward

I feel that I am very fortunate to have read all of these poems and even type some of them, although most of what I actually typed will appear in the next volume of Grandma's Poems. Through these poems, I had the opportunity to learn about a whole lifetime of love and loss, joy and remorse, and dreams and memories. As someone who loves and enjoys history, these poems are priceless in that through them I can venture past just a name and date and to the actual feelings about an important event in the life of a really important person. She may not have been a president or general, but she is my grandma, without who I and much else would not exist. Grandma June, thank you for letting us into your loving mind and soul.

~Melissa Magnuson-Cannady

Preface

These poems are a biography of my life, beginning in high school days when everything was so idealistic; later my time away from home in the Navy. There is a long blank time while I was busy just being a mom, just too busy to make life into rhymes.

Then came the grandchild, a divorce, a time to cry, to wonder; time to make rhymes to fulfill expressions too complex to keep inside. Later, here and there, came a few more, but when we joined the church, then came a time of happiness, which is all in these poems too. I expose my heart and my soul in many of these poems. Some have that twist of humor that is a gift to me; as well as my gift of gab!

A few I feel were not written by my hand alone, of which I am especially proud. They were truly inspired!

"Reason"

Gems of thought
Oft gather dust
Like iron wrought
They too rust!

"The Metamorphosis"

A dismal rain fell all day,
And cloaked the world in drab grey,
The earth was sheathed in a foggy blight
As Mother Nature walked that night.

Morn found a world anew
In each crystal drop of dew-
Shinning from its celestial place,
The sun shone on the fairy lace.

Each drop that yesterday was like a tear
Seemed suddenly to put aside all fear
And like some forgotten tale of yore,
Became a smile forever more!

Written the day Grandfather Huss was buried in Oak Lawn
Cemetery, Freeport, Illinois, January 30, 1939. It was truly one
of the most beautiful days I remember. The frozen twigs made
bells chime in the breeze. I was sure Grandfather was happy.
(John Huss: March 20, 1869-January 27, 1939 and his wife,
Mary (Veitmeier) Huss: March 4, 1873-September 27, 1949)

"The First Snowfall"
(High School Days, 1938-1942)

Down came the white feathery flakes,
Floating on the passing breeze
To cover up the frozen lakes,
And transform barren trees!

Hesitantly at first they came,
Like the first spring bird
Stealthily seeking some little crumb-
A description for which there is no word.

Finally, spurred on by happy faces,
Lifted in praises toward the sky,
They cover the earth with laces,
Such as no money could buy!

"Beneath the Willow"
(High School, 1938)

By the side of the weeping willow,
By the side of the rippling stream,
There lay an old man with arms for a pillow
Swept off in a pool of dream.

He dreamed of his happy childhood-
The mysteries of the old mill pond,
His wonderings through the wildwood,
And onto the world beyond!

The cool feel of water to his feet,
As he walked in the willow's shade,
The wholesome smell of wild wheat
As he passed through the wooded glade.

On, on, down memory lane he drifted
Through the years which had left their mark,
And his heavy old heart seemed lifted,
Into the light, from out the dark.

The old man was found where he lay,
In the shade of the old willow tree,
Where he had spent many a day
So that now with his childhood thoughts he might stay

Some goodly soul saw, and gently understood,
And in a white pine box they lay him away
Under the gnarled willow in the wood,
Where with his memories he might stay!

"A Mothers Prayer"
(1938-1942—High School)

As the old woman rocked in her chair
By the fireside, she recalled the day,
Which had turned to white her hair,
And chased all joy away!

The boys now homeward wended
And the world breathed a sigh-
For the yell, "War is ended!"
Was the universal cry!

At last came the memorable day
When the boys had sailed home
And vowed never again to stray,
From our beloved land to roam!

Haggard but happy they came
Marching to the beat of the band
Some were bandaged, some were lame,
Some less a leg, some less a hand!

She stood in the doorway and waited,
For the cheerful call of, "Hi, Mom!"
But she was told a message long-belated,
Which said her son was killed by a bomb!

So her son lies sleeping in Flander's Field,
Away from worldly care and strife
He never again a weapon can wield,
And he is gone forever from her life!

Oh, God, Keep our peaceful land from war
So that mothers may never know-
The sorrow that hers would be forever more
If her son to war should go!

"Dreams"
(Written while in the WAVES (U.S. Navy), 1943, Brooklyn N.Y.)

When the lights are out,
And you've gone to bed,
It's strange the thoughts
That spring in your head!

Little things they are,
So clear in the dark,
They seemed long forgotten,
But they've left their mark!

Sometimes it's the family-
The kids, and Mom and Dad;
Sometimes it's just a place;
Or some friend you've had!

Maybe you recall a face,
Or maybe just a smile,
At the time it seemed so little,
Now it's so worthwhile!

You lay and you think
Of things in the past,
They were everyday's happenings;
But they're the ones that last!

Now there's my Dad,
With his side-way grin,
Just a little thing,
But it's part of him!

My Mom's there too,
I can see her now,
Her one life's dream,
Is to own a cow!

Perhaps before too long
She'll have her dream,
But 'til this thing's over,
All she'll do is scheme!

When you're all alone,
And get feeling blue,
You just have to laugh,
At the pictures Joyce drew!

The door goes shut,
Paul tip-toes in,
He's late for supper-
"It won't happen again!"

Marjorie's growing up too,
And we fear that soon-
She'll set competition
For Joyce and June!

I see her in my mind
She's given up climbing trees
A "freshman" now in school,
She's wise about birds and bees!

One girl in particular
Talks of Bud and Bill -
If she remained single,
I'd love her still!

Trifling things they seem,
The ones that keep me awake,
All the money in the world,
For these I won't take!

The woods loom up in my mind
All quiet and serenity there!
It seems like an outdoor church
With the sermon still in the air.

Countless others like me
Have dreams like mine,
Memories that grow old,
And ripen with time.

Someday soon, we hope
We'll walk beneath the trees -
Thank God for America,
And get on our knees!

Until we see that day,
These dreams remain in my head-
When the lights are out,
And I've gone to bed!

"To Paul"

Darling, could I but tell you-
Of all the things,
Which in my heart I feel
That put my soul on wings!

Could I with words but match,
The love shone in your eyes,
Then my dear you'd know-
That I've found Paradise!

"The Farewell and Return"

(First verse written upon leaving La Crescent, MN to
Janesville, WI 1958. Second verse written upon the return to
La Crosse, WI 1959.)

Oh, where are the hills-
The rocks and the rills-
The beauty I once called mine?
Was it a dream
Or did it just seem
That Paradise
Is such a short time?

Oh, here are the hills -
The rocks and the rills -
Their beauty is once more mine!
And here I shall stay,
Until that day,
That God calls me home for all time!

"Progress"

(This poem was given to Mrs. Mills on the farewell to Hill Top School - 1969)

Good-bye little school
So high on a hill-
Lulled to sleep at night
By the Whip-Poor-Will.

Whose waking hours
Were filled with the joys,
Of laughter and lessons
Of girls and boys!

The time comes now
To say Adieu!
And so on this day-
We say to you-

Good-bye old era,
Hello to the new,
We only regret
Time's pawn is you!

"Clemency"
(1967 – 1968)

Today I wept a thousand tears,
A thousand tears for a thousand years-
For yesterdays with all their sorrows,
And broken dreams of all tomorrows,

Hope spring's eternal in each sigh,
Only to be drowned again in each tear I cry!
Oh sadness, you have possessed my soul,
Is self-destruction your only goal?

My hands are clasped in begging form-
For from a love all life is born.
Lead me, guide me, show me right,
Take away confusion - show me light!

There is no God - how can this be?
When with hope comes all eternity-
Oh foolish mortal, blinded by fright,
Wake up, walk on, feel His might!

As each dawn brings the new day,
And with darkness night fades away.
Yes, God is here - I feel his being-
Blindness no longer clouds my seeing!

With His hand on my shoulder His wisdom I share
My burdens are lightened with Him to care
Forgive me for doubting, for being so small-
Yes, give me Your hand, I will walk with You tall!

"Homemakers"
(1969)

Doris is a nurse,
And she's a real pro,
Helen can cook-
Oscar should know!

Betty's ambitious
In barn or cafe,
Kathleen has a brain,
She is at H&R Block today!

Bonnie can sew,
4-H she guides,
Pat has talent
On a keyboard she glides.

Bernice is content
With eggs and her chicks,
Grace can do anything,
Her works gives her kicks!

Lucy is smart,
Her children attest.
Mary's personality,
Is one of the best!

Elaine has patience
Job she outshines!
Edith remodels
For retirement pines!

Margaret's so busy,
On taxes just now.
Darlene is "Tops",
She'll show us how!

Elaine helps Harold
All chores she can do,
Lucille minds the store
But is a gardener too!

June envies these girls,
Their talents are varied-
Share your gifts, Homemakers,
Please the man she married!

Each has her own talents
Be they big or small!
Homemakers lets share-
With one and with all!

"My Church"
(1970)

A church need not have spirals tall
Or gold encrusted on the wall,
Mosaic windows need not be-
Or ornate altar for all to see,

Aisles need not have carpets laid,
Or pews of carved oak and velvet made-
A church for me is any place
Where to God I say my grace.

Arched trees a tabernacle make
And grasses green for kneeling sake,
A fallen log is just as good,
As any pew carved of wood!

A blue sky touched with sunset glow
Are windows through which heaven show,
Wind in trees and birds on wing
These are hymns no choir sings.

This is my Church where I pray-
Thank God for life and each new day-
For all who see who will only look,
The out-of-doors is the Holy Book!

The plan of God is very clear,
Who seeks guidance shall find it here.
Let your eyes be lifted high,
Let your soul rise to the sky!

"Tops Toast"
(1971)

We're the voluptuous ladies of Oak Ridge Hill
We've got lots of weight but little will!
We lose five pounds and then celebrate-
We lost the five and gained back eight!

Now some people we know just eat to live
A fortune for a metabolism like theirs we'd give
Others, like us, just live to eat-
We're the ones with the smile and big broad seat!

If we lose just 1/2 a pound a week all next year,
We'll be 26 pounds lighter when we next meet here.
Each must decide how much to lose and gage her loss
Now is the time for the head, not the mouth, to be boss!

Now we may be perfect women, but we all have one fault
When it comes to food, we don't know when to halt,
So at this Christmas time, I propose a toast-
Let's see who in one year's time can lose the most!

"Keith's Growing Up"
(Christmas 1971)

Christmas time has come and gone
And my poor wallet's flat-
Now it's time to return to school,
I can't say that I like that!

This year I was fourteen,
And so I got no toys-
It seems the fun of Christmas-
Is just for little boys!

Oh well, I guess I'll finish school-
So I can learn to be a Dad,
And someday my little boy,
Can have Christmas like I had!

"Keith's Talents"
(After Christmas 1971)

"Write a poem," the teacher said,
"Or illustrate one you like instead!"
I tried and tried, the results you'll see-
An artist I'm not, nor a poet will be!

Some people write at a drop of a hat-
I just proved no talent like that!
Others can draw with gifted ease-
I have no talent such as these!

I'm very good at fixing tires-
Mending fences and broken wires,
So let this end this useless try,
Edgar Allen Poe is not this guy!

"Hope"

Life they say-
Is a wonderful thing;
Sometimes I wonder-
But the flowers of spring-
Come after winter's thunder!

"Christmas Decoration"

Mother Nature spread her tinsel-
On the lowly weeds last night,
And in their sparkling splendor,
I knew the world was right.

As His eyes are on the sparrow-
So the weed must have its place,
So at this Christmas time
Stands proud with heaven's lace!

(Light reflecting on weeds when we took Lynnette to Joy's after
Xmas 1971)

"To Each His Own"

As does the song bird fly on wing,
So does the winter into spring.
And as spring gives way to summer glory
So now the fall bird completes the story.

Each time and place has its own,
And each cycle, birth to grown-
Does not man too, have his seasons-
And only God knows the reasons!

"Hear This"
(1971)

The tax notice came today-
I'll admit it quite a shock!
For on top of all the others,
This will really put us in the hock!

I told this story to the cows,
All standing in the barn-
That it was all up to them,
To make or break this farm!

No more free-loading-
I told that motley crew!
You've got a bigger job-
Than just your cud to chew!"

"When the summer was the hottest,
While you laid beneath the trees-
We worked and sweated making hay-
And hoped we'd catch a breeze!

Then we filled the silo
Nearly to the brim-
Hoping the battle of your bulge,
That silage would help us win!"

When the sun was at its hottest,
In August we cut the oats-
Hoped it wouldn't rain on the straw,
And gave up fishing time and boats!

We fought the autumn rain,
And prayed for a late frost,
Worked hard to get the corn in,
So it wouldn't all be lost!"

Now it's your turn,
To do us Farmers right,
So, Happy New Year to you-
And to you, a Good Night!

"Compensation"

The gutters are clean,
The straw is all new-
Now up comes the tails
Just like on cue!

First one, then another
Down the aisle they go,
Each has her method-
Some fast, some slow!

The job never ends,
You just begin all over,
If only they were on pasture
And eating clover!

Now the other end
Is just as bad-
You feed and feed,
And she still looks sad!

She blocks with her head
Your pitch fork of hay
Stuff she's refused-
All through the day!

She stretches and moos
For her neighbor's feed,
Especially with milkers on
She shows her greed!

18

She's helpless, seems hopeless,
She tries my nerves-
Her idea in life,
Is We are to serve!

In March we sow oats,
Plant corn in May,
Hope the harvest is good,
In July we make hay.

We work through the year,
In heat and in snow!
All for the cow-
That stands in the row!

She may seem stupid,
But she's one of my girls
She's just a cow to you-
But she's my string of Pearls!

With calf or with milk
She pays her way-
On our farms she does,
Just ask F.H.A.!

"Farm Wife"
(1972)

It's 9:00 AM
And I must say-
I feel I worked
Half the day!

I gave out hay,
Milked the cows
Bottled calves
Slopped the sows,

Had a tail slap
That really stung!
Had a loving lick
From a sandpaper tongue.

Checked the line
For suspected ills-
Dispensed 3 shots
And gave 5 pills!

Rinsed the milkers,
Washed them too-
Checked inflations-
Ordered new!

A string of cats
Got their milk
Makes their fur
Feel like silk!

Fed the horse-
She had her colt!
Said, "Hi" to mom,
She fed the goat.

The chickens too
Got their scratch-
Which reminds me-
I must fix that latch!

The geese got corn
The ducks did too-
This isn't a farm
It's a "Gol-Darn Zoo!"

I know I have
Many chores ahead
Before this gal
Hits the bed-

It's a darn good thing
I love this life
Because I am-
A Farmer's Wife!

"Quick Silver"

Today I looked at poems
I had written in days gone by-
I laughed at some, smiled at some-
And at some I had to cry!

The rhyme may not have been too good
About that I really do not care-
It was the thoughts and not the verse-
That I found mirrored there!

"Pawn"
(1972)

I kissed a little girl last night
As she slept upon my bed-
How much more that kiss would mean
If it came from you instead!

I try to understand
Why these things you've done-
And how you could have left her,
When her need of you had just begun!

I question myself-
And sometimes I almost know,
Then I look into bewildered eyes,
And all the reasons go!

She's become a little shuttle,
Between Grandmothers who love her so
Maybe they're all the Mother love-
This little girl will ever know!

I've tried so hard to hate you,
And cast you from my mind-
But I find that heart strings,
Very tightly bind!

I hope that someday you'll find
The tug of heartstrings too-
And l pray to God in Heaven
That it won't be too late for you!

"Reflections"
(Winter 1972)

This morning I realized-
Just how old I was growing-
For I raved and fretted,
Because it was snowing!

All I could think of
Was how I'd slip and slide,
Or stick the car in a drift,
And in general, freeze my hide!

Later, as I walked
Knee deep up from the barn,
I bewailed the fact
That I'm stuck up on the farm!

Now, tonight after chores
And I have grumbled all the day
I looked upon a scene of white
And overhead, a Milk-Way!

Suddenly, I was young again-
I no longer felt the cold -
I thought of games and skates and sleds,
My heart no longer felt so old!

It seems that as the years pass,
We're so busy living life-
That we overlook the little joys
That far outweigh the strife!

I resolved that from now on-
I'm going to live each day
With the joy I knew when I was young
And knew no other way!

"Revelation"
(Christmas 1972)

Today I put Christmas away-
In boxes and on closest shelves-
As I put them out of sight-
I hoped it was not reflective of ourselves.

We are so eager to celebrate His Birthday
With gifts and Yule-tide trim-
How much of this is just for show,
And how much because of Him?

"Self Pity"

Yesterday in despair I said,
"Death could come tomorrow!"
But throughout the day I took inventory,
And saw I had no sorrow!

"Winter Reign"
(1972)

Winter is staying long this year-
It covers the hills like an unmade bed,
And night winds sighing among the pines
Echo like voices crying in dread!

A lone windmill stands sentinel
A lost monument of days gone by!
Naked trees shiver and stand stark
Silhouettes against a western sky!

Winter is jealous even of the day
As the sun's rays she tries to spurn,
And rivals summer's day-
Opaque windows etched with ferns!

Everything is quiet and serene today
The world is a scene of white
Winter sits back to admire her work
For she vented anger through the night!

She is the dowager Queen-
Guarding her throne with regal rage
Knowing soon she must abdicate-
For Spring is coming of Age!

"A Mother's Heart Ache"
(1973)

Today I closed the door-
On my son's yesterday-
For rows of planes and model cars
No longer know his play!

Neatly catalogued the sample rocks-
The comic books and pistol guns-
Yesterday the world of a little boy,
Today, the memories of a son!

Where is that eternal line
That separates the two
Between the man he will become-
And the little boy we knew!

My heart cries a little-
And I ask God as I pray-
To grant that his tomorrow
Be happy as his yesterday!

"The Gift"
(Christmas 1973)

I took the tree down today,
It left me with a heavy heart-
For it seemed Christmas was over
Before it ever had its start!

All year long I planned-
Of gifts for each to give-
Now it's all over-
Did Jesus ever live?

Who am I to question
The wisdom from above-
To Him who gave His only Son
To us, His gift of love!

"Auction"
(March 1, 1974)
Gus Brosinski Auction

Auctions always seem so sad-
They seem to make me feel so bad-
For it is an era come to an end-
Of another farm, another friend!

The line of machinery, the pen of calves,
The earthy things a farmer has-
And in the barn, a row of cows.
Maybe outside, a shed of sows

And as each item falls beneath a bid,
I wonder how many tears are hid,
How many of the dreams come true-
Or how many plans, like mine, fell through!

"Acknowledgment"
(Fall 1974)

I stood at the top of my hill-
Yellow birch, golden maple, red oak and pine green
Colors of the hill and autumn valley,
Over all this, I am Queen!

To think that God gave me the right-
To call this hill my home -
Because where the autumn meets the sky-
I know there is another throne!

Thank you God, for the gifts you've given-
And forgive me for not always saying praise-
But in your infinite knowledge You know,
That my life is Yours all through my days!

"Ah Revenge"
(1974)

My master doeth nightly snore,
He keepeth me awake-
He maketh me lose my beauty sleep,
And causes my head to ache!

I beseech him to be still-
And calm his nightly roars,
And he swears to high heaven-
That he never ever snores!

Oh that I had a tape recorder,
To replay the snorts and groans-
I'd prove his nightly chorus
Is cause for broken bones!

At last I've found the solution
As I calmly go to bed-
For I put ear plugs-
In my little tired head!

Snore on, Sweet Prince-
I care not anymore-
I shall waken -with clear head-
And hope your nose is sore!

"Klutz"
(1974)

When in a hurry,
It never seems to fail-
I develop a pace
Slow, like a snail.

I'm all thumbs
Instead of fingers
With time an essence-
Each minute lingers.

Wings of Mercury
Are not mine-
My feet are lead
In the race of time.

"Ponderance"
(1974)

Thoughts run deep
Like rivers wide
A calm surface
Can torrents hide.

A face serene
Oft trouble shields
And clasped hands
A knife wields!

Beware the smile-
That hides hate.
Bold the fool,
Who tempts fate.

Know the truth,
Feel life's sting!
Pay the Piper -
Do your thing!

"Piggy "
(March 22, 1975)

Naked me!
Is sight to behold-
One thing sure-
I'm no centerfold!

Rolls of fat
And extra skin-
Plenty for me
And next of kin!

I just sigh-
And hide my sorrow-
I'll start my diet-
Yeah, tomorrow!

"Bulk"
(March, 1975)

The naked truth
Is plain to see-
I'm twice the woman
I used to be!

Not in my mind-
I wish were true-
But in volume
I pass for two!

"Emancipation"
(1975)

I am a liberated woman!
Now let me explain-
How I reached this status
And felt no pain!

I burned no bras,
Carried no cards-
I joined no pickets-
In neighbor's yards!

For years and years
I toted that pail,
A slave to the milk-line
It became my jail!

Each day found me
At a tiresome chore-
Scrubbing milkers and tank
'Til my fingers got sore!

With milking time
Now cut in half-
Machines do the work,
And I sit and laugh!

Pipeline milking
To my way of thinkin'
Is the farmer's answer
To Abe Lincoln!

Oh aching back-
And bended knee,
Gone forever-
I AM FREE!

With the Sta-Rite Panel
And the Dari-Kool tank
I'm the "Queen of the Ridge"
With Sorge to thank!

"Graduation"
(1975)

The last of the children
Graduates today
The last of five-
That have gone that way.

One more human,
On the "work-load" force.
In our kind of world-
Par for the course!

For eighteen years
We've tried to guide,
Now the rest of the road-
He alone must ride

If he needs our help-
We'll be near
He shall but ask,
And we will hear!

"Either, Or?"
(Winter 1975)

Today I clipped
All the cows' tails-
Soaking wet mops
From washing pails!

"Don't worry," I said
"My bovine beauties,
They'll be ready
For summer time duties!"

But now I find
Comes the rub-
Would I rather be hit
By a mop or a club?

"And Sins Will Be Washed White As Snow"

I walked on diamonds all aglow,
Reflected lights on fallen snow.
Myriads of them sparkled fair
Glistening silver patterns there!

Above as many stars shown down,
And joined the diamonds on the ground,
I stood amid the beauty there,
And had no doubt God was near!

I felt my sorrow begin to rise
Into open arms in lighted skies,
My broken heart felt whole again
For His love forgives all sin!

"Farewell to Summer"

Today across the azure sky
I heard a lonesome song-bird cry,
The sadness of that winsome call-
Said, "Farewell to Summer, Hello to Fall!"

Where has the summer gone so fast -
And why can't those days forever last?
As time is such an evasive thing,
So days fly by, like birds on wing!

"Departure"
(Passing of Gust Brosinski, neighbor)

A stern handsome man
Asleep before the dawn-
Surrounded by the loved ones
And those whom he has spawned!

Alone, but dutiful to the last
Tear faced, yet erect, stands his wife,
Accepting condolences,
And praise for all his life.

I weep inside for you,
My heart aches in rhyme,
My prayer asks God to heal
Your loss, and dear neighbor, -mine!

"Choice"

Spring has sprung
And I've begun
Again to writing verse.

Now I could sing
Because it's Spring
But that is even worse!

"Night Writer"

When the Spirit moves me,
I am forced to write-
How come he does this
In the middle of the night?

While most people are sleeping
And having sweet dreams,
My mind is wide awake,
And rhyming various schemes.

I should just fight the urges-
And let Morpheus run the show,
But those rhyming verses -
Just won't let me go!

I might just as well get up-
And take a pen in hand-
A poet laureate in night gown
I am at your command!

"Plea"

Winter – did you have to come so soon?
It seems only yesterday it still was June
I'm not ready for your snowy flurries,
  For icy roads and blowing furries!

Couldn't you have waited yet awhile,
Before your white blankets start to pile?
I had so many plans for fall,
I'm just not ready to heed your call!

Go ahead and have your fling,
Just don't forget there's always spring!
And I shall escape your wintery ire,
  Cuddled by a roaring fire.

"Persistence"
(Summer 1975)

Hello, Dear Cottonwood,
With branches so tall-
You made it, you made it,
In spite of it all!

Many times you were broken
And branches torn off-
In my book of life
You were a loss!

As a sapling you were trampled
And cut to the ground-
Once you were even
Just a grassy mound!

One year too,
A horse split you in half-
You were put together
With a homemade graft.

I look at you
And your welcome shade-
We humans are fools,
But you are God-Made!

I see in you Cottonwood
As not only a tree
But an example of hope
That you give to me-

So wave your leaves proudly
As flags in the sky-
You deserve all your glory
For you wouldn't say die!

"Oh No!"

Heaven forbid
If my talents been hid
And I'm a Grandma Moses!

Not with pencil and paint
Of Scenery or Saint,
But with limerick and proses!

"Spring"

I looked at the terrible mess
And I wondered why-
I'm sure it didn't look like this
Last year on the Fourth of July!

"Appearance"

The face of a clown
Is just painted on-
When the grease paint goes
Is the clown gone?

"Life"
(1975)

Our plans are all in shreds-
And hope seems vanished too-
Then we gather up the threads-
And re-weave a pattern new!

"Nudity"
(Summer 1975)

A little snake-
Did change his clothes-
Right there beneath,
My rambling rose!

I know because
I found his skin!
He was out,
But it was in!

"The Circle"
(Fall 1975)

Today I saw the hills
Covered with a patchwork quilt
And the valleys too were filled
With all the harvest gilt!

Was it only yesterday-
That everything was green
And the earth seemed covered
With a silken screen?

And I know that tomorrow,
Before I waken from the night
The world will turn again
And it will be all white!

And through all the stages
Each season in its turn
I'll wait the most for Spring
God's promise of return!

"Ah Me!"
(Fall 1975)

Some women have crow's feet
Beneath their eye-
I've got the whole bird,
And half of the pie!

The middle age spread
Came to me ten-fold-
Why must I grow fat-
Along with "old"?

My feet have enlarged
I now wear size ten-
I know I'll never
Fit that size eight again!

The slacks that I wear
Are really so big-
A few years ago-
I'd have fit in one leg!

My bra too
Has grown in size,
If I were a cow
I'd bring a prize!

My hair is all colors
And streaked with gray-
When I was younger
I'd planned it that way!

I eat two meals
When I begin-
One for my mouth,
And one for my chin!

My only consolation
When I look in the glass
Is that the woman I see
As a "Grandma" will pass!

"Germination"
(1975)

Some people think
In a straight line
But when I think
It seems to rhyme!

This may be an asset
I just don't know-
But at least my thoughts
Get a chance to grow!

"Turnabout"
(Spring 1975)

Yesterday all I did was complain
About the mud and muck!
A result of the first Spring rain-
In the middle of which I was stuck!

Well, Mother Nature heard my call
And last night she froze the ground
And put a white cover over all
Now I make another sound!

We humans are hard to please
I'm sure the elements find-
When Mother Nature tries to appease
We are of another mind!

43

"The Clown"
(1975)

One day someone said to me
"You've sure got a sense of humor,"
I wonder what they would have said
If they knew it was just rumor?

It's a good thing my face doesn't mirror
At times what I feel inside
And the jokes that bring out laughter
Are just a cover for my pride!

Why burden the world with my troubles-
And the things that bother me-
It's better to make one person smile
Than to have the pity of three!

"Fever"
(Spring 1975)

Oh what a mess are the days,
Of the first big Spring thaw-
With the cover of winter melting
And the winds so wild and raw!

All the earth now seems to be mud
Everywhere streams rush to make rivers,
Miniature lakes and ponds cover the roads
While above the trees tremble and shiver!

It is hard to believe that all this
Was left here since last year-
It is the wakening time for all
For Spring Fever time is here!

"Ah Ha!"
(1975)

Just think-
When I am dead
You'll remember
Things I've said!

Maybe you'll forget-
That's all right too!
I'll just take my gift for gab
And will it all to you!

"Our Pride and Joy"

Lynda is bright and shiny
Ever so quick to smile–
With her enthusiasm,
Even the sternest she can beguile.

Paul seems so serious
But underneath it he is fun,
And the stories he can tell
Especially with a gun!

Brad just loves to tease–
But fishing is his thing
How he hates that he must work,
When his soul wants to wing!

Kathy is the farmer
The tractor is her car,
With that brain of hers,
She can go so far.

Keith works the farm
He has a sense of humor,
He needs it to work with Ma and Pa,
That he loves it is only rumor!

"Happiness Is"
(March 1, 1976)

When my husband whistles
It's the same as my song—
No matter how he puckers
It comes out all wrong!

I know the tune in his head
Must have a lovely ring—
But when it hits the outside—
That is another thing!

His whistle means he's happy
And that thought makes me glad—
So whistle on, dear husband—
It really isn't all that bad!

"Recognition"
(was published)

My cake pans are bent
They've seen their best days,
But they've served my family-
In oh, so many ways!

They came to the table-
They went to bazaars,
If they weren't filled with cake,
Then it may have been bars!

They served at wakes
Weddings, anniversaries, showers too,
Sometimes they were decorated
With pink or with blue!

They've gone to picnics
And even the FAIR-
They stood with the best
In the judging line there!

They're battered and bent-
They deserve the Purple Heart!
But I like them better
Than new from K-Mart!

"Popped Buttons"
(For Jerry Veglahn after the birth of Tammy 8/15/1976)

Now every Dad
Must have a son –
That is a standing order!

But have you seen
A prouder man –
Than when he has a daughter!

48

"Dear Daddy"
(Forever and Ever)

(Published in the Rockford Register Republic on June 9, 1977)

A blanket of snow lies on your grave
But I know you're not really there-
Because I saw you yesterday-
In your easy chair!

I saw you sitting there
With your head cocked to the side-
And the TV program you were watching-
Made you smile wide!

Today you stood at my door
And told me to be glad-
And not be unhappy anymore-
For you'd always be my DAD!

"Gone, but not Forgotten"

You are gone
And the night is long –
Even more so than the day

The hours drag by
And I could cry
Because you are away!

49

"Christmas Card"
(1983)

When I was a city girl
And I got a Christmas card,
I envied pines and hills,
And snow on a country yard.

Now I live among the hills,
And the snow covers my trees and yard.
So when I send Season's Greetings,
I am inside my Christmas card!

"Decade"
(10 years, Oak Ridge Homemakers)

It was ten years ago,
Our Oak Ridge Club began,
A group of neighbors,
And a Homemaker's plan!

A lot of us then
Had children in school,
Now a whole new generation
Learns the "Golden Rule"!

Our lives have changed
In these years gone by.
Births, weddings and funerals,
How the time does fly!

We've shared the joys
And each other's sorrows
For that is what life is –
Thank God for tomorrows.

Weathering storms together
Isn't just a farmer's strife
But what makes people love another
It's the baling-twine of life.

We're not only a club
Or a neighborhood clan
We're friends forever,
With the Master's Plan!

May the first ten years
Be just one stepping stone.
Of our Oak Ridge club
For God, Country and Home!

"Spring Fling"

A spring fling
Is a dance in school-
But in our barn
It's another rule!

A Spring Fling
Is a rummage sale-
In our barn
It's "Duck that Tail"!

A Spring Fling
Is something that's flung-
In our barn-
It's juicy cow dung!

A Spring Fling
Is a great big splash
That comes propelled-
From our cow's behinds.

"Randy"

(November 13, 1977)
(Killed in a car accident, November 11, 1977)

A bell tolls
From a tower,
And echoes in
The hills above.

People stand
At a graveside-
In mourning
And with love!

A whisper echoed-
From the sad
Down the hillside-
Too bad – Too bad!

"Remorse"
(About Randy)

I no longer have to worry
About how much you drink-
Or leave the light on for you
Above the kitchen sink!

I no longer have to fuss
About your long blonde hair.
Or the dark whiskers
That are growing there!

I don't lie awake to hear
The motor of your car-
Or listen for you to close the door
And not leave it ajar!

But all these things and more
I would gladly do
If God would only
Let me tell these things to you!

"Evolution"

The golden leaves
Have turned to brown
And with each breeze
They tumble down-
To cover earth.

The summer sun
Too has gone
And cold rains
Drown Robin's song!
Fall is here!

My blond hair
Has turned white
My step now heavy
Once was light-
I am old!

I don't care
Because I know
Spring still comes
After snow-
And time passes on!

"His Will"
(For Judy Pedretti, February 10, 1984)

I cry not for you who left-
Because He called you Home!
I cry for those who love you,
And now seem so alone!

They look at me through tears-
That fill bewildered eyes,
And my heart breaks for them,
For I have no answer to their "why's?"

If my arms around your shoulders,
Or my kiss upon your face
Helps to ease your sorrow-
It's only through His grace!

If I could ease each heartache,
By letting you know I care-
Then I'd know my reason for living,
Is because God put me there!

"Detours"

Each night
I ask the right
Road the Lord wants us to go.

It seems 'til now
It's been wrong somehow-
And the detours have been our woe.

I cursed today
For each delay
That plagued the way I chose.

Then I thought-
This could be wrought
To show the rightful road.

I have the sign
His help is mine-
For He will share the load!

"The Color Green"

*(Poem was sent to Quillin's contest and won a prize,
March 14, 1986)*

I love green!
Green is great

In the winter
I love its glow
When its Holly
And Ho! Ho! Ho!

When Holly green,
Is mixed with lime
Then it's a SHAMROCK
And soon Spring time!

In the summer
I love the sheen-
When all the earth
Is colored green!

And in the fall
With the sky so blue
Green turns to gold
I love that too!

I love green
In all the seasons
It's my calendar
For all these reasons!

I love green
Green is GREAT!

"Expose"

I come home from a party
All shiny and bright-
I looked like a queen
If just for tonight!

First off come the heels
I wiggle my toes
Feels good, the freedom
From those panty hose!

Off comes my hair
With one little tug
My chic coffier
Was naught but a rug!

My teeth come out too,
So I can see what I clean,
Just soap on a brush-
No need to use Gleem!

Without my bra,
I'm surely let down
I'm no Dolly Parton
In an old night gown!

Off comes the girdle,
Let it all hang out
The freedom is grand
And I leave out a shout!

Now the real me
Is ready for bed.
Oops, first remove the glass
From my little head!

Ah, now that's better,
I feel so at ease.
Behind closed doors,
Where no one sees!

"To Helen"
(Helen Soucheck, August 30, 1987)

So you are eighty
It can't be true!
For if anyone is ageless,
It has to be you!

What is a year
But a mark of time.
The body grows older
But not the mind!

Wrinkles are there
That is true,
The credit of time
Earned by you!

So, Dear Helen,
Enjoy your day,
Be happy forever,
In God's way!

"Hurrahs to Ma's!"

Are you tired of hearing-
How young you look,
How spry you walk,
How good you cook,
How smart you talk?

What do they expect,
Those who say these things-
Shouldn't you show it
If your heart has wings?

So keep flying high
Enjoy every day-
Forget the birth years-
You are here to stay!

"Promise"
(To Joyce on the day she climbed her mountain,
October 22, 1988)

Yesterday I climbed a Mountain,
Which foolishly I called, "Mine."
But when I reached the top-
I knew that it was "Thine"!

All I surveyed below me,
Including the home I love,
Would never have been possible,
Without your guidance from above.

Oh give me this time on earth
To enjoy all you have to give.
And I will know in my heart-
That my Lord will ever live!

"Resurrection"
(Rhonda Wrobel Lilyquist funeral, October 29, 1989)
(The sun's rays fell on the family and casket)

We stood upon the hillside
Come to say the last "Good-Bye"-
I looked across the valley
Into a grey and cloudy sky.

I felt the sadness all about me
Filling every space-
And across the grass between us
I saw your saddened face!

I looked again into the sky
Now an azure blue.
And saw the rays of sunshine
Were reaching down to you!

And while my heart was saying,
"Oh, Dear God, why?"
I heard the voices praying,
"Before we live, first we must die!"

"Just a Little Longer!"

Oh Lord, I have so much to do-
Before you call me home-
People to see, places to go-
And your beautiful land to roam.

So please prolong our meeting-
Of that promised day-
So that I can appreciate
Your heaven here on earth today!

"Preview"

I stood on my hill
Known as "Mountain High,"
And saw where the land of God,
Meets the country of sky.

I thanked the Lord
For the privilege given-
Of this meeting on earth
Before our meeting in heaven.

"Always, Forever"

I stood at the top of my hill
Which I call "Mountain High"-
And gazed at the glowing beauty
Of silhouettes in a western sky!

The valleys below are patchworks of green,
Mixed with yellows, reds and tan.
I'm overwhelmed and awed-
Helpless to express with eyes of man.

I take a deep breath-
As I say a silent prayer
That when time dims my eyes,
This beauty will still be there!

"Harvest"

I look in the yard
And what do I see?
That's not a partridge
In the pear tree!

I see ducks and turkeys
An old fat hen-
Some guineas, a rooster
And none in a pen.

They pick my grass,
Eat all my plants,
Nothing is safe-
Not even the ants!

Their sharp little eyes
Miss not a thing
The only thing safe
Is the bird on the wing!

Eat on, feathered friends,
Get nice and big –
You'll fit my freezer
Instead of a pig!

"Angels"

I believe in Angels
They're with me everyday
I believe in Angels
God sent them here to stay!

I believe in Angels
They help God with his task
I believe in Angels
They comply with what I ask.

I believe in Angels
They don't always grant my plea
I believe in Angels,
They know what's best for me.

"Holiday"

Most people wait for the week-end
As a time for fun and play.
I wait for the week-end
Because the bank is closed today!

My bills have outrun my cash,
And pay-day is a week-a-way
I hope that by some mistake
No one will cash a check today!

Will that day ever come
When I can rest at ease,
And enjoy my week-end
With no "over-drawn" fees!

"Homemakers"
(25 years, December, 1989)

Twenty-five years ago
When we formed this club,
We all had small families
And houses full of love.

As time went along
Throughout the year,
We've shared with each other
Through joy and the tear.

We've lost some members
But also gained new,
Each one so welcome
We hope you knew!

Once we were neighbors
And also best friends,
Now we are sisters
Whose love never ends!

"From the Heart"
(Published in "Echoes of Yesterday"
The National Library of Poetry, 1994, Page 460)

Write a poem-
Someone said,
I know you've got one
In your head!

I can't I said,
You don't understand-
You can't write poetry,
On command!

Rhyme and reason
Must have a goal-
Without these things
It has no soul!

Before a poem
Can have its start
It must first begin
Within the heart!

"Hibernation"
(Thoughts in the barn, February 17, 1991)

I'm exhausted
And I've just begun the day-
Is it my mind or body
That I feel this way?

Have I reached stagnation
Or is it winter's cold
Am I all at rest,
Or just growing old!

I'll call it hibernation
And now comes the rub-
When I awake in Springtime-
Will I have a cub?

"Substitution"

This time the scientists
Have been at it again-
Now it's pork-
That has known no pen!

They made that "substitute"
"The other spread"!
But there's nothing like butter-
On a piece of fresh bread!

There's a stand-in too
Even for beef-
The things it's made of
Are beyond belief!

The cheese market now
Has a non-dairy disguise
If you're looking for taste,
It's not very wise!

Now all you scientists
With your unlimited talents
Why don't you let Nature
Alone with its balance?

Instead you should concentrate
On the ultimate goal
Of finding a substitute
For coffee, gas, oil and coal!

"Amen"
(March, 1991)

A country church among the hills,
A sentinel defying time-
The eternal home of generations,
Which proudly now, I call mine!

There is a man God has chosen
To be his spokesman here on earth-
We thank God for him
That he was chosen for our church!

With his sermon or his song
His voice fills the air-
He must herold angels,
As we feel their presence there!

I've heard the sound of music
From the greatest of them all.
In churches called cathedrals,
With spirals high and steeples tall!

Saint Patrick's of New York City,
The Crystal one out west,
Of all the organ music,
To me, ours sounds the best!

Maybe it's the organist-
With her gift from above,
But I'm sure the sweetness of the sound,
Is because it's played with love!

The Mormon Tabernacle Choir,
Or the greatest of St. Paul-
Can't rival our own chorus
They are the dearest of them all!

Sometimes the things we take for granted-
We don't credit for its worth,
It seems we have but a small preview,
Of God's Heaven here on earth!

"Decision"

What if when you go to bed
You've had your last day,
And on the morn you'd meet the Lord,
Whatever would you say?

Would you have to turn you back,
Or could you look into his face,
Have you had salvation?
Or fallen from his grace?

If how you would turn is a question,
Then tonight as you pray
Ask the Lord for direction
And grant you yet another day!

Untitled 1

Do you give thanks
For prayers answered
Or do you just complain
For those withheld!

"There is Love"
*(Maggie (Paul), Wanda, Joyce, Mom and myself on the trip to
say Goodbye to our dear Aunt Dorothy)*
(March 22, 1991)

*Years have passed
Since we met last,
But it seems yesterday!*

*The things we did
From parents hid,
We know now was our play.*

*Hair now white –
Once was light,
But that is nature's way.*

*We talk of things,
Pull old heart strings,
And so goes the day.*

*As we travel
Lives unravel-
We have so much to say!*

*Miles fly,
Time goes by-
We are on our way.*

*Old hurts healed
New love revealed –
It's Aunt Dorothy's Day!*

"April Fool!"

The yard is white,
And I'm uptight-
I thought that it was spring!

I was fooled,
Got over-ruled-
Winter is still King!

"Awakening"

In the spring
I become prolific,
Not always good,
Or terrific,
But from the heart!

Like the blossom
In the twig,
Thoughts burst forth,
Small and big-
I am happy!

"Memories"

*(Written for the mother-daughter luncheon at church,
April 3, 1991)*

*I have so many memories-
That make me feel glad,
The older I grow, the more I know
You were the best I could have had!*

*You were always there for me,
To guide me through the day,
You soothed my dreams at night,
And joined my childhood play!*

*You taught me how to stand
Long before I could walk,
You taught me how to sing
Long before I could talk!*

*Sometimes I doubted your wisdom
And thought I knew best-
Now I know with time
That it was just a test!*

*We became as children
Sharing all things in love-
Time and age had no meaning,
For we were blessed from above!*

*There was a time not long ago
When you led the way,
That was when you took my hand
And taught me how to pray!*

*Later, when you became tired,
We reversed the stand-
It is now I will help you,
And I who will take your hand!*

Someday you'll have to go
Because He'll call you Home,
But I'll have so many memories
I'll never be alone!

I love you Mom!

"Grandmother"
(Written about Mark Magnuson, age 16 months, April 9, 1991)

He has two mothers
This grandson of mine-
One is his real Mommie-
I am just part-time!

She's the one who bore him,
And then there is me-
She'll have him all her life-
But he is mine, nine to three!

I can love him, I can kiss him,
I can hold him tight-
But when he's crabby,
He goes home at night!

"Talents"

Mom does her thing with paint and brush,
And Joyce does hers with thread,
I have no talent such as these,
So I use ink instead!

Mom's scenes rival nature's own
Joyce's quilts and pillows win at the fair
My poems are mediocre-
But they reflect my thoughts there!

Sister Marjorie writes prose and rhyme,
Hers shows much sophistication-
But when we compare the two
We can not deny we are relation!

Brother Paul just sits and laughs,
He neither writes nor sews-
But when it comes to story-telling
He can beat the pros!

Daddy was our inspiration-
He applauded each step we could rise,
I'm sure he is very pleased,
As he sees with angel's eyes!

"False Face"
(Thoughts from a magnifying mirror, written April 9, 1991)

*My face is full of wrinkles
And crevices deep as fjords,
My neck is like a turkey's-
It shows all the cords!*

*Lordy, I am homely
My mirror doesn't lie!
Oh who will put my make-up on-
Whenever I will die!*

*I hope my sisters out-live me
So they can do the job-
Otherwise I want the casket closed,
Let them think I am a snob!*

"Common Denominator"

*I'm no poet laureate,
And I'll never be-
Because the things I write
Come only from me!*

*I'd like to write of lofty things,
Of country and of nations,
But the only experience I've had
Is on the farm and my relations*

*They are the common things
I know this is true,
But when I write them down
I hope that they give joy to you!*

"Housewife"

When I go to bed at night
My house seems fairly clean,
But when I see it in the morning,
It's another scene!

Where did this mess come from-
I don't think its right
There's got to be some gremlin here
In the middle of the night!

I guess I should clean my glasses
Before I sleep at night-
Then I would be more prepared
To greet the morning light!

All day long I'll cook and clean
And try to mend my way-
My only consolation
Is my benefits and pay!

"Man of God"

(Given to Dorothy Halverson and Steve Jensen (pastor) after funeral of Dorothy's husband)

I saw a depth beyond your eyes
Into your very soul,
And a love from deep within
That very few know!

Through your love, you minister
And become a brother in their pain-
Each time He calls someone home,
You see the Cross again!

It's the love you give to others
When they are deep within His need-
You become their Savior,
But I can see you bleed!

I can hear the heartache,
Beyond the joyous sound-
And I know, though here on earth,
You are Heaven bound!

"Ghost Writer"

I feel a depth of perception
That often denies explanation
As if someone else
Holds my pen in expectation!

What mysteries are in my sight-
Am I to write some great solution
Or just be some fool
To try again for evolution!

79

"Geometry"

"Summer's right around the corner"
That's what we said-
But a corner is right angles,
That's why we got snow instead!

If summer was a straight line-
Between two points in a ring,
Then we could alibi the thunder-
Along with the snow we get this Spring!

"Spring Cleaning"

The cows are shedding
And I am dreading
To have to milk today!

Itching eyes
Worse than hives-
Hair is everywhere!

Each spring
It's the same old thing-
They shed their fur on me!

When they change coats,
I'll take goats
Because they are smaller!

"Discretion"

I pray to God to help me
Because my life is such a riddle,
He can see the beginning and the end-
While I only see the middle!

I'm sure He catalogues my prayers,
And when He gets the time-
He first takes care of important ones,
And then considers mine!

Mine may not all get answered
Although I might think they should-
But he sees the picture over all-
Only He can judge for me what's good!

"Destination"

I never know
When it's the end
Until I get there!

You won't either
So take neither
Until I show you where!

"Resolution"

My poems are very simple
They are not at all complex,
They come from me only,
And never from a text!

My mind is a reservoir,
And the outlet is my pen-
It seems to be commanded,
Of what to write, and when!

My husband thinks I'm milking
When I'm with him in the barn-
Little does he know
My thoughts are miles from the farm!

They are here and there,
On other days and other times,
Of things past and future,
And in general, making rhymes!

Maybe something will come of it
And I'll have made a poem-
Then again, I might just milk,
And keep my happy home!

"Friends"

The preacher came to call today
And caught me in a mess!
I had just come from the barn-
No time to change my dress!

The floor needed to be swept,
There were dishes in the sink-
"Oh my Lord," I said out loud,
"What ever will he think?"

Then a thought came to me
From somewhere out of the blue,
"He hasn't come to see your house,
He has come to see just you!"

It's true I said,
And my face lit up!
I asked my friend to come in
And share a coffee cup!

(I'd still like a 10 minute notice!)

"The Artist"

Creation must have an outlet
Or it dies within the seed-
Far better to grow a flower
Than to fertilize a weed!

"So There!"

I think I live in Weed-Land,
As that's all I seem to see!
The more I cut and pull-
The more they laugh at me!

They poke their heads above the grass,
And hide among the flowers,
It must take them just minutes to grow,
To remove them takes me hours!

Sometimes I think I'd like an apartment,
With no lawn at all to mow-
Then I'd buy plastic flowers,
And sit and watch them grow!

"Practice"

Why is it so difficult to say, "I'm sorry"?
Especially if you are to blame!
Or for someone to say, "I love you,"
When you know they feel the same.

If you can tell the Lord, "I love you,"
Or say "I'm sorry for the things I do."
Then to tell those here on earth
Will be much easier for you!

"Trick or Treat"

The Halloween pumpkin
Who stood on guard-
Against goblins and witches
Out in the yard,
Looked surprised and bewildered
With his cap of snow-
Where on earth did Autumn go?

He looked surprised
And so did I-
Who would have thought
There was snow in that sky?
It had looked like rain
Or maybe some sleet-
It was Mother Nature
Who played Trick or Treat!

"Stepping Stone"

I have a sidewalk to nowhere-
But once it had someplace to go,
Why or where it went,
I guess I'll never know!

The end is covered now with grasses
Like someone's unkept hair,
And I sit and wonder-
Whose footsteps once passed there!

Were they children's happy ones,
Or lovers hand in hand,
Maybe they were slow like mine,
Or with a cane and some old man.

Did they walk the straight and narrow,
Or get lost along the way-
Was there someone to guide them there,
Did they know how to pray?

So I sit and I wonder,
Of days and times that are past.
Although the footsteps are long gone
The sidewalk seems to last!

"Union"

We are kindred souls
You and I-
Although we walk different paths,
Mine is all believing
Yours is asking "why?"

"Murphy's Law"

The auger broke-
The tractor is heating
Running late-
Cancel that meeting!

"Good Bye Old Friend"
(Nels Johnson's funeral – June 3, 1991)

Today I took a trip
Into my yesterday,
I saw where I once lived-
Remembered where I play.

The road is now cement.
And the little town a city,
The trees have all disappeared,
In their stead, hi-rises, what a pity!

I came to say "Good-Bye"
To my childhood friend.
I remembered our old oath,
To be buddies 'til the end!

I looked into a face
Of an old man now gone-
Where is that young man I knew,
In a mirror, I see I went along!

Time ever passes,
New replaces old
We pass this way but once-
An old story, now retold!

"Fall, 1991"

It started snowing
And it kept going,
All through the month of November!

Now I'm quite old-
Or so I'm told,
But this is the worst I remember!

It used to snow
But come and go
And never stay 'til December.

I guess I'll just hush
Learn to say "mush,"
And address myself in Alaska!

"Master of None"

I run the parts department,
I'm the official "Go – for – Girl,"
And in between these jobs,
I give housekeeping a whirl!

I am the white-haired milkmaid,
The Grandma babysitter-
When the kids play ball,
I make a great pinch-hitter!

My kitchen is the meeting place
Where daily plans are made,
Sometimes we have a salesman,
Sometimes a broken blade!

I never know when I begin
How many I will feed,
Who knows how many apples grow
From a single seed?

I am a farmer's wife,
A job I wouldn't trade-
Each experience I have,
Is another memory made!

"Feeding Time"

I fed the barn today-
The calves and cats and dogs,
I'm glad we sold the pigs,
Or I'd have to feed the hogs!

To say I don't mind the chores
Is a pack of lies,
The ones I hate the most to feed,
Are those dog-gone pesky flies!

They are so unappreciative,
They don't care where they lite,
They use me for a landing strip,
And where they lite, they bite!

I make plans for their demise
My scheme is now two-fold,
Those who don't succumb to the sprayer
Will soon die of the cold!

"Best Friend"

My sister is "perfection personified,"
In her house, her car and dress,
She totally denies this plateau,
And claims it is "a mess"!

If my mess were twice as bad,
I'd never have to worry,
And when the unexpected guest arrived
I'd never have to scurry!

I'd just sit back and enjoy myself,
And never ever think
About the dust upon the floor,
Or the dishes in the sink!

They say that opposites attract,
I hope this is the case
Because she is my best friend
So my faults she can erase!

"With Branches Wide"

It's lonely time again
Everyone has gone home-
I sit among crumpled gift wrap,
And feel so alone!

Yesterday all their smiles
Rivaled tinsel on the tree
Now they are all gone-
And it's just "old lonesome me"!

I look at the gifts given
With love from each heart,
And as I caress each one-
I feel the tear drops start.

I thank God for my family,
And friends who all love me,
And hope they will return next year
And share my Christmas Tree!

"Fall Bouquet"

The last plumes of the Pampas Grass
Waved "Good-Bye" to me,
So I picked them and put them in my bouquet,
For all my friends to see!

"My Grandfather Clock"

My Grandfather Clock
Stands all day long-
And each quarter-hour
Sings out his song!

Most of the time
I'm not even aware-
Of the sound of the song
He sings from there!

Sometimes I stop,
And just stand still-
To enjoy the song
Like the Whip-poor-Will!

But when the night-time comes
That I can't sleep-
He screams so loud,
That I could weep!

Every fifteen minutes
He lets me know-
And every hour that passes,
And it goes so slow!

Now daylight has come
Revenge is mine-
I'll turn him to "Silent,"
And just use the time!

"Healing"
(Pastor Steve Jensen used this as part of Paul's eulogy,
April 16, 1994)

Winter's thaw
Exposes earth,
Last night's fog
Today's rebirth!

Frozen crystals,
Cover scars-
A lacy blanket,
Filled with stars.

God's promise
In rainbow hues,
Man-made scars,
His love renews!

"Early Risers"

My foolish lawn
Started turning green-
Because a winter rain,
Made a stream!

The blades of green
Poked through the snow,
They were so sure,
The snow would go.

Surprise, surprise,
Winter's back,
And the blades of green
Have all turned black!

They'll rise again
When it's really spring.
But for now let's say
They've had their fling!

"Me"

I have rebellion in my soul,
I resent any kind of conformation!
Freedom in thought and deed are my goal,
Rather than a set regulation!

Maybe I was born too late,
Or maybe much too soon-
Whatever is my fate-
I am Me, Woman, Known as June!

"Cocoon"

A sugar coating on the ground,
Shimmering ice on trees-
Stalactites from the overhang,
What beauty rivals these?

Weeds made into lace,
Car windows opaque with frost,
Words defying description
On these sights are lost!

I'll take the four seasons,
So I can enjoy the change-
How boring would life be,
Like a song that has no range!

"In the Eyes of the Beholder"
(Sent to Pastor Jensen in answer to "baldness")

If bald is beautiful,
Can having hair be homely?
If what a person perceives
Comes from the eyes only-
Then how sad is the world!

It's how we feel
In our inner soul
That to see beyond the surface
Should be the goal-
Then joy is ours, and all things are beautiful!

"Enjoy"

Life is boring-
How can this be,
When the world is filled
With so much to see?

So much to see
So much to feel,
Half of it imagination,
The other half real!

To be bored with life
Is just a condition-
Brought about by lethargy
And lack of ambition!

Life is a state
Of things inside-
Give it freedom,
Don't let it hide!

Feel all things
Both happy and sad-
Let your heart sing
And you'll feel glad!

No time to be bored
Or be discontent!
Live as you should
Like the good Lord meant!

"Sharing"

I wrote a poem,
I read it twice-
I had no one to listen to it
Or ask advice.

Did it sound all right,
Or was it too cold-
Did it make one happy,
Or just feel old!

The things I write of
Are all part of me-
They come from my heart,
Or what I see!

The reason I write them
Is I want to share
The things I feel
With you who care!

"Harbinger"

I love to see the sunrise
Reflecting on the snow,
And all the icicles,
Take on a rosy glow!

The yard is filled with rhinestones,
Cotton candy coats the trees,
Lacy weeds make music,
In the early morning breeze!

Just last month it was darkness
At this time of day-
My heart is filled with joy-
Springtime is on its way!

"Collections"

My husband and I
Are collectors of things-
There are eagles and angels,
And cherubs with wings!

There are lamps and plates
Dolls, dishes and cars,
There are clocks and books,
And old canning jars!

We haunt flea-markets
Rummage sales and auctions too,
At some discount houses,
We even find new!

Our only hope
Is that when we depart
That the things we collect
Will find a new heart!

"Daydreams"

I'd like a week of Sundays,
Instead of just one day.
I'd like the time to rest,
Or indulge in some light play.

I could enjoy the leisure life,
And put aside my cares,
I could have a picnic,
Or recline in my lawn chairs!

Maybe we could take a ride,
With no plan in mind,
Or tour some forgotten place
And discover some new find!

Since my dream is out of reach
I'll just take my one day,
And cherish every moment
Until I get my S.S. pay!

"Decisions, Decisions!"

I swear I live in "Mudland"
For it is everywhere-
I know how it gets on my boots,
But how'd it get in my hair?

Even the lawn is soggy
As I go to check the rose-
I sink into the grass
Right up past my toes!

Now comes my decision,
At this point I don't know-
If I'd rather have this mud,
Or another foot of snow?

One is as bad as the other,
We are too anxious for perfection
That what Mother Nature gives us,
Is always cause for reflection!

"The Frugal Shopper"

I went into the grocery store,
And then I gave a sigh-
How come the food I like
Is so dog-gone high?

I'd love some pork chops,
Thick meat upon the bone-
But in order to make that purchase,
I'd have to sell my home!

A thick steak would taste so good-
Again it's out of sight,
To display it in the case,
It's temptation, that's not right!

How come potatoes are so cheap
Is it to appease my soul?
Am I to forget the meat I love,
And eat the potatoes whole?

They are full of carbohydrates
They help keep my diet in line-
Oh, I wonder if they'd let me buy
The meat I want on time!

If we only didn't have to eat,
Think of all the money we could save,
Better yet, think of the bank account
If I didn't buy what I crave!

I suppose if I were a millionaire
And money was no thought,
I probably would never care-
What my money bought!

But since I am on budget,
I'll just have to bide my time,
And when those goodies go on sale-
I'll be the first in line!

"Beyond the Surface"

If cleanliness if next to Godliness,
Then I'll never see the Throne,
Because no matter how I try,
This never describes my home!

If the bedroom is spotless,
Then the kitchen is a mess,
Or if the kitchen is spic and span,
Then the living room is in distress!

I wonder if I'll ever see the day
That all things are in place,
If I do, I wonder,
Will I be welcome in His Grace?

I hope it's just a saying,
But if it's really true-
Then I hope the cleanliness of my soul
Will come shinning through!

"Futility"

Yesterday I was in the "Executioner"
When I said, "Off with their heads!"
No, my Dear, they weren't people,
Just Dandelions in my flower beds!

Their green leaves were like spiders
Spread wide in all direction,
But it was the little yellow flower
Which was cause for my dissection!

The yellow polka dots upon my lawn,
I must admit are really pretty-
But the million little seeds they leave,
Is cause for murder, that's a pity!

They can hide all through the summer
But are the first to rise in Spring,
They seem to grow from every crack-
Their crown of gold makes them king!

I know it is a useless task
To exterminate this earthy weed
They must have some unfound use
But for now I'll concentrate upon the seed!

If I could find the secret
Of how it outlives a freeze,
And apply it to our alfalfa stand,
Then to become a millionaire would be a breeze.

"The Chosen"

When those we love have a cross
That seems for them too hard to bear-
And in our heart we question,
"Does our Savior really care?"

Then I say, "Satan go from me-
For it is just a test
To find those special Angels
Who can help the Lord the best!"

For they shall sit beside Him
As they've seen Hell on Earth,
And because they know what pain is,
They'll have proven to Him their worth.

Because they've known the heartache,
The blackness and the dread,
Their hearts shall help lift others,
For with God there are no dead!

"Ah, Sweet Mystery" or "Rodin"

When something is profound
It throws my mind in thought,
Of the "Do's and Don'ts" of life,
And what I "should and ought!"

The "Whys and Wherefores" of my questions,
Is what I continually ponder,
Will I ever find the answer-
I have cause to wonder!

I wish my mind would go to sleep,
And all the questions would be still
How come the consternation
Goes on without my will?

Sometimes I find the solution,
But again, it may elude my mind-
The only consolation,
Is the answer comes in rhyme!

Does this mean I am a poet,
I have much reason to have doubt,
But it is one way to debate
And get my answer out!

"Mom"

An empty picnic table
Sits beneath the old pine tree,
Once it was laden
But now it's empty, like me!

When I had my children
My heart knew it was full,
Now that they've each gone their way,
It's me who feels the heart strings pull!

I don't ever question
That their love is still mine,
But sometimes I don't see them
And the days between seem such a long time.

From the time they say "Hi-Mom"
To their last "Good-Bye"
Our joyous time together
Makes the hours fly!

When the house is once more mine
And the voices all are still,
I'll sit alone with my memories
To enjoy the hours that they fill!

"The Test"

Of those who say they love me-
If I died before the morrow,
How many would stand in sham,
And how many in true sorrow?

"Lethargy"

What happened to my mind?
There seems to be no line of thought-
It is difficult for me to understand
What I do, and what I ought!

I know I should be productive,
And at least do something right-
It seems I've reached a lethargy,
I am the same from morn to night.

Maybe I am in a cocoon,
And a metamorphosis is going on inside,
Perhaps when I awake
New thoughts will be my guide!
(I'll have wings on which to glide!)

"Trust"

I am an open book
For all to see
For what I write on paper,
Exposes all of me!

But when I look at you
You seem to want to hide,
And I never ever feel
You let me come inside!

Where is your trust?
Is it you, or is it me-
Why don't you come outside,
And let the world see!

108

"Interpretation"

You questioned my faith
From out of the blue-
From the scriptures you could quote-
To prove my way untrue.

You put me in a shock-
My mind put up a guard-
I had taught you life's value,
Now you call it a charade!

My belief is all spirit,
While yours is from law-
Which way is better
It's not ours to call.

We must each believe,
In our own way,
Only God knows the answer
It's not for us to say!

"My Prayer"

Lord, you have given me miracles
When I asked for none-
All I ever wanted,
Was to be forgiven by your Son!

Now, I need a miracle,
So to you I send this plea-
Please dear Lord,
Keep those I love safe for me!

Untitled 2

A child runs,
And tries to hide-
A child runs,
A child dies-
WAR

"Intersection"

I am in the middle of my universe
As it is the same in all directions-
No matter where I am
I am at an intersection!

"Choices"

When you are standing in the middle of nowhere,
You are an equal distance to somewhere,
And an invitation to go anywhere!

"Trial"

Lord, this time you gave me a mountain
With no paths on which to tread,
As I look at the darkness before me
I am filled with an ominous dread!

The summit that reaches above me
I know is bathed in sunshine there,
And I will reach that plateau
Because I am in my God's care!

Meanwhile, my feet stumble,
As I grope for your hand in the dark,
Oh Lord, come walk beside me-
Guide my journey as I start!

"Church Bell"

A bell tolls,
Angels sing-
A call to God
With each ring!

From the valley
Across the hill,
The bell rings
Never still!

His house is open
For all who hear,
His love is ours-
Vanquish fear-

A bell tolls,
We give praise,
He is Lord God,
All our days!

"Wedding Bell"

A bell rings
Angels dance,
All God's children
Love romance!

Candles burn,
Hearts entwine,
The Holy Trinity
Forever bind!

Smiles abound
Tear drops too-
Best wishes expressing
Just for you!

A bell sounds,
Angels sing-
Two people together,
A wedding ring!

"Toll Bell"

A bell tolls,
Angels cry,
Another soul
Says "Good-bye"!

Good-Bye to Earth,
With all its strife,
Good-Bye to Earth,
And mortal's life!

Hello to Heaven-
The meeting place,
Where we see God,
Face to face!

A bell tolls,
God calls us home,
Now with the Lord,
No more alone!

"To the Window above the Sink"

I thank the Lord for many things
As the day rolls by,
From the dawn's first light
And the sunset's glowing sky!

When I am doing dishes
And get a chance to think,
That's when I thank the Lord
For the window above the sink!

I remember many things
From my vista there,
And it's far more rewarding
Than from an easy chair!

While my hands are in the soapsuds,
I've watched the seasons fly,
From the first Robin to the Sno-bird-
Their full flight and first try!

I've seen the bushes bare and naked,
The drive filled with snow or mud-
The same bushes green and flowering
And the trees with their first bud!

I've watched our children catch the bus
And later their children too,
Through my window I've seen the rain,
And days with skies so blue.

Some days it's tractors pulling seeders
When spring was on its way,
Other days it was a parade
And wagon loads of hay!

What do people do in apartments
With a blank wall to stare-
Oh God, give me that window,
So I can have the world to share!

"Card on Hand"

We could have got you a prettier card,
If we had gone to the store,
But our thoughts would have been the same
Even if it would have cost us more!

"Reflections"

When the mirror reflects only emptiness and
you see no one you know no matter where
you roam-
It's time you look in that mirror and
see who you are are the people around
you - then it's time to go home!

"A Rose is a Rose"

I was shoveling snow
That was boot high
And keeping a watch
On an ominous sky.

I hoped my back
Would stand the strain
And I secretly wished
It would have been rain!

I stopped for a rest
And to wipe my nose,
Then I saw it there-
One single red rose!

It was poked up above
The blanket of snow
That covered the planter,
And made quite a show!

It was plastic, of course,
But I didn't care,
A promise of springtime
Was just for me there!

"Worth"

I put my make-up on,
I comb my hair,
I add some ear-rings
With no one to care.

I match my sweater
With my new slacks,
When I look in the mirror
All I see is cracks!

My face is old
Just the eyes show life,
Once I was a bride,
Now I'm "the wife."

My husband is sleeping
In his easy chair
I wonder if he knows
Just how much I care?

I say I dress myself
Just to please me
But the truth be known,
It's because of He!

Maybe when he wakes up
He'll say I look nice
If he does that,
It's my reward as wife!

"This Day"

I woke with great expectations
Of what the day will bring,
And the thoughts of anticipation
Makes my heart to sing!

The seconds turn to hours,
The hours become a day,
My hopes of some great elation
Begin to fade away.

The night has brought on darkness,
The day has gone on by-
It seems nothing great has happened
And so I give a sigh!

But as I fold my hands in prayer
I must thank God for this day,
I pray he will forgive me
For living life my way.

Give me my belief in tomorrow,
Let me be grateful for yesterday,
For the joy in anticipation
Is the game we adults play.

Let my hopes spring eternal,
Always let me have my dreams
That way the hum-drum day
Will be better than it seems!

"Set Back"

What do you know-
Three inches of snow,
It's supposed to be Spring!

Mother Nature is fickle-
She still likes to tickle
The buds and flowers she'll bring.

Just a little more cold,
Enhances the gold,
And makes the birds wing!

The flowers will rise,
Give praise to the skies,
And my heart will sing!

"Rehearsal"

When we were farming
And things went wrong,
We'd pull ourselves together,
And just go along.

Sometimes we'd say,
"I can't take it anymore!"
But it always seemed
We got up off the floor!

A farmer it seems,
Always lives with strife,
It's part of his day,
A part of his life!

Now we're retired,
Farming woes are gone-
Time for song and celebration,
We thought so — Wrong!

Our problems now are medical,
Not at all what we dreamed,
Life is like that,
Not at all what we schemed.

We'll take each day we're given,
And look tomorrow in the eye,
Thank God we're still farmers
Who never will say "Die"!

"Signs of the Times"

When your stride becomes a "shuffle,"
Or your walk becomes a "toddle,"
And you can't blame medicine,
Or too much of the bottle,
Then it's "Old Age"!

When your backside becomes a "butt,"
And your tummy becomes a "belly,"
And all things have gone "south" but you
And all parts shake like jelly,
It's, "Old Age"!

If you ask for the "Senior Citizen Rates,"
And the medicine chest if filled with just that,
To cover thin hair you have to wear a hat,
You've reached "Old Age"!

If you prefer to stay at home,
And you'd rather sit than walk,
If you like the quiet better than the talk,
Then relax and enjoy-
You've earned "Old Age"!

"My Time"

I love the morning
When everything is quiet,
And I sit with my thoughts
Or the dreams of the night.

I can sit in my chair
But walk memory lane,
When I was a child,
And life was a game!

I am a school girl,
With my very best friend,
The secrets we shared,
Makes me smile again.

I remember the picnics,
We didn't need swings,
We were happy as larks,
With just Nature's things.

There were family vacations
At just a small lake
A week in heaven
Our pleasures to take!

The boys that I dated
I can think of them all-
I'm glad that I married
The one named Paul!

We had five babies,
Each such a gift!
They are all grown now,
Time is so swift!

Our "five" turned to "ten"!
We love them all the same,
Half are from others,
Half carry our names!

I think of our grandchildren
When they were so small,
Now some of them are married,
And some grown so tall!

Now the household awakes,
I put away my pen,
When the marrow returns
I'll remember again!

"Awakening"(2)

Little birds begin to sing,
Tiny trumpets herald spring,
Branches burst with swollen bud,
Children's feet encased in mud!

Sidewalks get swept with brooms,
Mother cleans the storage rooms.
Green now outshines white,
Days are longer than the night.

We dare again to dream
With the coming of the green,
Life has a brand new start
From deep within the happy heart-
Spring is here!

"Points of Light"

Inquiries come in,
In person and phone,
"How's he doing?" And
"How's your day?"

I give out answers,
All filled with hope,
They listen with hearts,
And say, "We'll pray"!

We thank God
For friends like these,
Who give joy to the day,
And shorten the night!

Gladly we accept
Their thoughts for us
For each prayer becomes
Another point of light!

"Permission"

If you have to leave me,
I would let you go-
Not because I want to,
But because God says so!

When He'll call you Home,
Only He knows the time,
Then you'll be "His"
While now, you are "Mine!"

Yes, I'll be sad,
Because you'll be so missed,
But I'll content myself
Because you'll be "Heaven-Blessed"!

125

"Beyond the Sunset"

I'm alone now,
But it's ok,
Because I know I'll see you,
Each and every day!

I thought when you left,
I would not fill my day,
But I've found you everywhere,
Especially when I pray!

How can I be sad,
When I know you're all right,
Knowing you can breathe again,
With ease, through day and night.

Of course I miss you,
For together we are one-
And I'll not be whole again,
'Til we walk beyond the sun!

"Spirit"

I try to visualize you
In your easy chair,
But try as I may,
I can't see you there!

Then I try to see you,
As you sat by the table,
But try as hard as I can-
I'm really not able!

I have asked God
To make me strong,
So 'til we meet again
The time won't seem so long!

This must be the answer,
From God to that prayer-
You can't be anyplace special,
Because you're everywhere!

I can't miss you
Because you're not really gone
Your Spirit is with me,
Through the day and all night long.

Your love is everywhere,
It fills my every day,
You are with me forever
As promised in God's way.

"A Thankful Mom"

You kids came home this Sunday,
Because it was our wedding day,
You come not to celebrate,
But show love, cause Dad's away!

It would have been our 48th,
Many years in any life,
But what is time when you're in love,
And was a happy wife?

Dad is gone but not forgotten
You proved it one more time-
Your love was freely given,
Reflecting all of yours, and also mine.

The garage got a new roof,
The cars will now be dry,
Your work was done together,
If I could, I would cry!

Your gift was oh so needed,
I accepted with a heart of love,
I know Dad too smiled with acceptance,
In his home with God above!

"Thirty Years of Love"
(Thirty-Year Anniversary of Homemakers-1994)

Thirty years, three decades,
A lifetime ago-
What a pleasure
Each other to know!

Caring and sharing
Each other's lives,
Makes us better people,
And much happier wives!

Our love and hugs
In joy or in sorrow,
Helped each other to know
God promises tomorrow!

Once we were neighbors,
Always were friends,
Now we are sisters,
Helping hearts to mend-

We are "Oakridge Homemakers"
A name to be proud
Joined together by love.
Oh, what a crowd!

"The Answer"

Another crisis hit my life,
Another jolt to a widowed wife,
Oh my Lord, what will I do?
My only hope is to count on you!

I said these words, alone, out loud,
And as in prayer, my head was bowed.
I could see no answer hard as I tried-
In my heart, my soul cried!

Before the day came to an end,
God sent to me a long lost friend.
The friend gave me an answer to my prayer,
And once more I knew my Lord is there.

"Soon"

"I shall go first-
To prepare you a place-"
I knew your promise,
It was on your face!

And so you left me
To go alone,
The smile on your face
Said you had gone Home.

I'll finish the things
That you left undone-
Then my Darling
I'll meet you – beyond the Sun!

130

"The Wait"

Here I sit,
All alone,
With the TV remote
And the telephone.

I have hope
Someone will call,
If not for me
But to talk of Paul.

The TV plays on-
The phone is quiet,
The usual happenings
In a widow's night!

"I'll call you,"
Promises made
The longer Dad's gone
His memory fades.

I'll make it somehow
I pray to be strong
'Til I'm back with Paul
Won't be so long!

"On Eagle's Wings"

No wonder I don't see you
In your easy chair-
You're flying now with the eagles,
Free, My Love, in God's care.

"Habits"

How long will I sleep
On only half of the bed-
And not sleep in the middle
Like I could instead?

How long will I sit
On only my place at the table,
And not sit where you sat
Because I'm just not able?

How long will your chair
Sit empty and stare
At my place on the davenport
As I sit there?

I'm a creature of habit
Who will go on sharing
The every day things
And never quit caring.

How long is long-
Is there a meaning to time?
After 48 years
Memories of you will always be mine!

"Reunion"

Today I looked loneliness
Straight in the eyes.
And the stare I got back,
Made me cry!

It's the day after day
Followed by night
That go into months,
That give me the fright.

The echo of footsteps
In an empty room,
The sound of clocks ticking
Add to the gloom.

I take a deep breath
I must go alone-
God give me strength
'Til you call me Home.

I try to be brave
So no one will know
That sometimes I wish
Tonight I could go!

So I paint on a smile
And wipe away the tears-
Lord, I pray,
Don't let it be years!

Untitled Thought

How long can Eternity be when
life on this earth is just the dash
between two dates on a grave stone.

"Motion"

I am a whirling Dervish,
I keep spinning like a top-
That way I keep busy
So my world will never stop.

If I ever stop the spinning
And the turning ceases too-
Then I'll be no more free,
Than a monkey in a zoo.

A day would never pass
If the world failed to turn
And life would be a bore
With nothing new to learn.

So, I'll keep on moving-
Filling empty space with time,
Eventually one will meet the other,
And all worlds will be mine!

"Rest"

Mind-
Go to sleep,
No more bleep
Until the dawn.

Thoughts –
Go away
Tomorrow is another day-
Come back.

Dreams-
Fill nightmare's space
Another time, another place,
Mind's vacation!

Hope-
For all tomorrow
Entwined joy and sorrow-
The thread of life.

Death-
Farewell to strife
End of life,
Welcome, Land of God!

"Prayers Answered"

My heart felt broken,
I couldn't believe the pain-
My family was shattered,
How could it be whole again?

The rift seemed insurmountable,
How could it ever heal?
My life was in shambles,
It seemed so unreal!

My thoughts were about my hurt.
Many times in my day
I found myself with clasped hands
Asking guidance as I pray.

Oh, please Dear Lord, hear me-
Help my daughter in her grief,
Let me Lord, understand her
Give my heart relief!

Give me that understanding
That only you can give-
Now I thank you Lord-
A further proof that you live!

"It is Ended"

The windows of the old barn stare back at me, and in their emptiness, reflect my own loneliness. Tall silos pierce the sky, echoing the pigeons' call of "Look at the goon!", further intimidating me. They call it as they see it, even the birds have their opinions!

Where have all the cows, the calves, their sounds, the milkers pulsating, silos unloading, the hustling, ever busy invigorating times gone? Where have all the "could have been," "used to be," and "should have been" gone? Gone with my youth, our kids, their chatter, and my husband's strong straight back! To the land of dreams gone sour, to hopes crushed, to the future filled with disparity.

The fields lay fallow, only the trees whisper to the pond, "where are the cows?" God alone knows my feelings of futility, I miss my farm!

The line of cows, the new hay, the smell of silage, the hum of tractors-the busy days. Gone, all gone in the closed book of my yesterday. Now only the ticking of the clock in empty rooms, fill my day.

Thoughts run rampant in my head that used to brag of its keenness, and catalogued efficiency! A situation I never thought would happen did, and a new word is in my vocabulary, called "boredoom"!

I know it was time to go, but the time of passage is never easy. The mind belies the aging body, and the slowing of "the reaction time." It is easy to look backwards and say, "if only," or "maybe we could have!" I must content myself with "this is it," and try somehow to accept that which now seems unacceptable.

There are things needed to be done, things I know I should do, but I have no interest in doing them. My incentive has become unresponsive, gone to sleep like the rest of my body. Seventy candles tells me I have earned my "R and R." Now I must make my mind listen to the body. Like the old horse put out to pasture, like the fields let to fallow, now it is my turn, please God, let me accept it gracefully.

"November Thoughts"

A few stubborn apples hang on barren branches, defying all laws of gravity. Dried stalks of hollyhocks stand stiffly with seed pods hanging and a few plumes of pampas grass make flags against a cold north wind.

Leaves dance and swirl, forming mountains and valleys where they catch and pile. Birds are feather balls sitting on fence lines, silhouettes against a grey sky. Cattle stand in a permanent hunch. A thin layer of ice covers the water tank!

The dog looks wistfully at the porch, and waits for an invitation to come in. The cat had a change of mind as he dashed through the opened door into November and did a mid-air pivot to return to the warm house.

My husband and son look like sequestered monks, dashing hither and yon doing chores in hooded jackets and gloved hands.

The tractors rebel, sputter and choke, give off a column of smoke as they finally start. I sit bundled in a sweater and winter slacks, repeatedly checking the thermostat. I can't seem to get warm today! I count the days on the calendar until April – it seems like a year 'til then.

These are the dark days of November. Maybe that's why we celebrate Thanksgiving Day, lest we forget life can be wonderful, God is with us, and in December is Christmas!

"We"

Here we are, just you and I, alone, in a house loud with silence. I look at you and see how deeply lined is your face— where has that young man gone? Then I look in the mirror, and I see he has left with the young woman who once was me.

I wish I could say they are all the traces of Smiles—but I can't, for I have traveled with you over the miles that have left their imprints there. They are our merit badges!

We now have completed the circle, we are alone, together again, as it was in the beginning. In the chambers of our hearts echo and re-echo the sounds of years of love, joy, sorrow and yes, tears of being parents. From babies to woman and manhood it has been our honor, privilege and obligation to know and share the lives of our children. Now we are alone.

I don't mind the quiet, for it is rather an award for time earned, and there will be many hours yet to share with those who are of us.

You raise your eyes and they meet mine, we say no words, but our instant of togetherness is timeless, it is now, was always, and ever will be—for it is called love.

Appendix:

A collection of writings about my grandpa and grandma and life on "Mountain High Farm" written in high school.
~Melissa Magnuson-Cannady

Melissa Magnuson
American Literature
September 3, 1998

Grandpa's Coffee

I remember my grandpa like it was just yesterday that I last saw him. As he hugged me with his strong arms made from years of manual labor, his tender smile lighted up his aged face.

I remember a story he would tell me quite frequently. First his eyes would light up like the tree in the living room at Christmas time and the little village of miniature houses that my grandma would always set up near it. Then his eyebrows would arch up in to the seemingly never-ending forehead. He was bald with brown, white, and gray hair forming a horseshoe around his head. Then he would begin.

"When you were two, you would always drink my coffee. All I would do was walk the couple feet to the toaster to get the waffles for us, and when I got back, all my coffee was gone." Then of course, grandpa would innocently ask me "Where is my coffee?" in that special voice he used for talking to us younger grandkids. And I would giggle—I knew that I had stolen his coffee successfully and had drank it all.

Then he would smile again, with those lips—small, but with a bigger bottom lip than upper lip. However, there was not a hint of a pout, as far as I could see. He would get up. Not as fast as he could have in his better years, but he completed the task just the same. And with his hands pour some more coffee; or pick up my little baby brother. His hands—soft and comforting, yet showing evidence of him bringing in the harvest for so many years. Now they contained a network of rivers and tributaries running over his worn skin.

Years later, I sat there next to him in his hospital bed. Listening to his now unsteady breathing. I thought about how kind and giving he had been. I looked at his ears. They were long and wrinkled and I thought about all of the trillions of sounds that bounced off of them and to the beating drum inside. I was wondering if he could hear me if I cried and said, "I love you." Now I look back and wonder if I knew that it was the last

142

time I really had to say those words. I think about those blue, blue eyes. Crisp and clear as the sky on a sunny day in summer.

And I remember grandpa and the coffee story today. Grandpa drank the coffee of life, but this time, God took it away, so that they can drink coffee together up above.

Melissa Magnuson
American Lit. M-3
October 5, 1998

My Loving Grandpa

My grandpa was the kind of person who you would meet and never forget. First of all, it would be hard to forget his bright, crystal blue eyes. His personality was equally unforgettable. His caring attitude, friendly smile, and loving heart were not easily forgotten.

He lived through The Depression of the thirties. Though he was very young, his mind contained memories of living and getting by with very little. Therefore, he appreciated more of what he had in life and didn't take anything for granted.

World War II, in which he was involved, shaped his pride, not only for his country, but for his family as well, and gave him responsibility. After being a gunner in a fighter plane, he took on the challenge of more responsibility and became the secretary to the colonel. After the war, he and my grandmother eventually moved to a little farm outside of Stoddard, which they later named "Mountain High Farm." Here, many years of manual labor and being exposed to the harsh elements of freezing cold temperatures, and the sun, humidity, and scalding hot weather have aged him. It was these harsh conditions that helped mold and give his face, as well as his body, the expression-filled characteristics that I remember him having.

The hand that was used to drive tractors and feed and milk the cows was used in tender ways also. He used them for shaking hands, giving hugs, and cutting up waffles into miniature bite-size pieces for my brother and me to eat during breakfast with grandpa and grandma at the farm. I can just picture grandma and grandpa sipping coffee and watching *Regis and Kathy Lee*, while still making sure that we didn't choke on any food or make a mess, as kids are generally inclined to do with fluids, such as milk, or something sticky, such as maple syrup.

Having the patience to tenderly cut my waffles or to not get too upset when some farm machinery broke was one of his many gifts. His ability to show emotion was another one of his many gifts. No matter what kind of mood he was in, he could always show them—sadness, happiness, anger, annoyance, or contentness. Not very many people show their emotions constantly. Many try to hide their true emotions from others. Grandpa didn't do that.

While in the hospital for cancer, he showed many emotions—joy, weariness, loneliness, sadness, and hope. I was glad to see the hope in his eyes, expressions, and movements. Many people would probably give up the hope for staying alive, but not Grandpa. He enjoyed life and enjoyed being with his family and friends too much to leave before his time.

During his battle with cancer, while he was at home, he would sit in his big, comfortable chair. He would sit there all nice and warm during the bleak cold winter.

Now during Christmas time, when I go over to my grandma's house, I sit in that old chair and think of grandpa. As I look at the lights on the tree and study the little miniature village that grandma always sets up, I think of how his eyes sparkled when he was joyful and would start to water when he was sad. All of a sudden, I realize that my eyes are starting to water too. I am glad that I am able to show my emotions like my grandpa did. I hope that I also inherited his giving personality too, so that I can be the loving, caring, and gentle family member and friend to so many—like my grandpa was, and will always be remembered for.

Melissa Magnuson
American Literature
September 16, 1998

A Day at the Farm

As a child, I would go over to my grandpa and grandma's house with my brother while my mother was at work. We would go over there four days out of the week, and go to a day-care the other day. At the time, I liked day-care because of other kids my age; but now, looking back, being at the farm was probably more relaxing and enjoyable.

After rising each day, we went over to the farm. We would go in the old farmhouse until it became unbearably boring, then we would head to the barn. The cool morning air was always so refreshing. It woke me up like a cup of coffee would wake up grandpa. The scent of the barn is a mixture of so many things: the sweet yet musty smell of hay, the dusty smell of the grain, the general smell of living animals. And of course, the pungent smell of manure was present as well.

In the barn grandpa would move down the aisle slower than my father, but of course his age affected his quickness and agility. He, like a lot of elderly people had a slight limp. However, once a cow got out, or something of that nature happened, it was almost like he traveled back in time, to a time when he could really move. Then I would look again, and he would appear to have returned to the present and slowed down to his normal pace.

After the milking was completed, we all took the short walk up to the house for breakfast. Waffles with butter and syrup, cereal, and milk fresh from the bulk tank usually made up our menu. And, of course coffee, which I stole from grandpa. We would be sitting around the kitchen table and as soon as grandpa got up to bring us the waffles, I would take a big swig of his coffee. I would try to drink it very quickly—they believed that caffeine wasn't the best thinking for a little child to have regularly. He would sit down, and after he had cut my waffle into tiny bite-size pieces. He would try to take a drink of coffee only to realize that it was all gone. He turned his head slightly

146

and looked directly at me. I would, of course, try to hide my guilty smile, but it slipped through. He would smile, and tease me about stealing his coffee. He then got up and refilled his cup. We would finish breakfast and then the ritual of daily chores would continue.

Grandpa and dad would go and cut hay. Because of safety reasons, I wasn't allowed to ride on the tractor very often. Once in a while, I would get to. The wind rushing past me, whipping my hair about, the smell of fresh cut hay, bugs buzzing about, and grasses swaying in the wind—it was all very picturesque.

With what grandma and grandpa called "Magnuson luck," something would usually break, and on to Viroqua we would go. Grandpa liked vans—big, comfortable, and painted shades of brown. At the Nelson Agri-Center, they would get some parts, while my brother and I would look at all of the toys longingly. Of course, being as grandpa was—a grandpa who spoiled his grandchildren, he let us each get one small toy. Since it would now be early afternoon, we went to eat. Country Kitchen was a favorite; breakfast all day, and placemats that we could color on. Grandpa would smile at us and his eyes would twinkle. He would laugh at me because I would often get a cinnamon roll—he loved sweets just as much as I did.

Soon after we returned to the farm, mom would be there to pick us up. Grandpa liked seeing his daughter-in-law, but he was rather sad after seeing us leave. After the nightly milking and chores, the house would seem as empty and hollow as a rotting old log in the pasture—we had filled it during the day with yelling and playful screaming.

At the time, I probably didn't appreciate life with my grandparents on the farm in the country. I didn't understand how wonderful the simple ways of life were back then, the gentle breeze comforting me, the scents soothing me. I am glad that grandpa and grandma had this farm where I could experience all of this at a young age. When I am alone, in the cool breeze of summer, I secretly thank them for all those "Days at the Farm."